The Little Book

# The Little Book of
# Confident
# Children

## JOHN GRAY

**V**ermilion
LONDON

First published in 2001

3 5 7 9 10 8 6 4 2

Text © Mars Productions 1999

First published in the United Kingdom in 2001 by Vermilion
an imprint of Ebury Press
Random House
20 Vauxhall Bridge Road · London SW1V 2SA

Random House Australia (Pty) Limited
20 Alfred Street · Milsons Point · Sydney
New South Wales 2061 · Australia

Random House New Zealand Limited
18 Poland Road · Glenfield · Auckland 10 · New Zealand

Random House South Africa (Pty) Limited
Endulini · 5A Jubilee Road · Parktown 2193 · South Africa

Random House UK Limited Reg. No. 954009

Papers used by Vermilion are natural, recyclable products made from
wood grown in sustainable forests.

A CIP catalogue record for this book is available from the British Library.

ISBN 0 09 188217 6

Designed by Lovelock & Co.

Printed and bound in Denmark by Nørhaven Paperback A/S

# Contents

# A Short History
# of Parenting

When parents make mistakes in parenting it is not because they don't love their children but because they just don't know a better way. The most important part of parenting is love and putting in time and energy to support your children.

Without an understanding
of their children's needs,
parents cannot effectively
support their children.

When their hearts are open and
their will is nurtured they are
actually more willing to co-operate.

You have to learn how to listen so that children will want to talk to you. You have to learn how to ask so that children will want to co-operate. You have to learn how to give your children increasing freedom and yet maintain control.

To be a better parent it is not enough just to stop doing things like punishing or yelling to control your children. To give up manipulating your children with the threat of punishment to maintain control, try to find other equally effective methods.

Our children's problems begin in the home, and can be solved at home.

To be a better parent it is not enough to stop doing things that don't work.

To cope with changes in society parents need to change their parenting approach.

Likewise, if parents want their children to be able to compete in the free world, they must prepare their children with the most effective and modern approaches to parenting.

Western society is now organised by the principles of freedom and human rights; parents still use parenting skills from the Dark Ages. Parents need to update their parenting skills to raise healthy and co-operative children and teenagers.

To give up old ways of parenting, new ways must be employed.

Ironically, from the perspective of positive parenting, nurturing a strong will is the basis for creating confidence, co-operation and compassion in children.

The goal of positive parenting is to create wilful but co-operative children.

They do not lie or cheat because it is against the rules, but they are fair and just. Morality is not imposed on these children from outside but emerges from within and is learned by co-operating with their parents.

Rather than seeking to create good children, positive parenting seeks to create compassionate children.

Past parenting approaches focused on creating submission; positive parenting aims to develop confident leaders who are capable of creating their own destiny, not just passively following in the footsteps of others before them.

# The Benefits of Positive Parenting

Confident children are not easily swayed by peer pressure nor do they feel the need to rebel.

They think for themselves, yet remain open to the assistance and help of their parents.

The intimidation of yelling and spanking no longer creates control but simply numbs a child's willingness to listen and co-operate.

The threat of punishment only turns children against their parents and causes them to rebel.

Punishment in the past was used to break a strong-willed child. Although it may have worked to create obedience it doesn't work today.

Most importantly, punishment and the threat of punishment break down the lines of communication. Instead of being a part of the solution, you the parent become a part of the problem.

Punishment makes you, the parent, an enemy to hide from instead of a parent to turn to for support.

Unless they are free to ask for what they want, children never clearly learn what they can get and what they can't.

When given the freedom to ask for what they want, children's inner power to get what they want has a chance to blossom.

There is a big difference between being manipulated by a whiny child and being motivated by a brilliant negotiator.

Positive parents maintain
control throughout every
negotiation and clearly set limits
on how long it can go on.

By giving your child permission
to ask for more you give that
child the gift of direction,
purpose and power in life.

Without a strong sense of self, people will even be attracted to abusive relationships and situations, because of feelings of unworthiness and fear of asserting their own will.

Adjusting one's will and wish is called co-operation. Submitting one's will and wish is obedience.

Giving children permission to feel and verbalise their resistance when it occurs not only helps children to develop a sense of self but also makes children more co-operative.

It is not healthy for children to follow their parents' will mindlessly or heartlessly.

Obedient children just follow orders; they do not think, feel or contribute to the process. Co-operative children bring their full self to every interaction and thus are able to thrive.

Positive parenting practices seek to create co-operative children, not obedient children.

Co-operative children may still want what they want, but what they want most is to please their parents.

Giving children permission to say no does not mean giving them more control; it actually gives the parent more control.

# Why Children · Become Unruly & Disruptive

Each time children resist and the parents maintain control, the children are able to experience that mum and dad are the bosses.

When children are misbehaving or not co-operating they are simply out of control. They are out of your control.

When children begin to feel the thrill of being the boss they also begin to feel very insecure and demanding.

To restore co-operation a parent
needs to regain control through
picking them up and moving them
into a time out. God makes children
little so that we can pick them up
and move them.

Rebellion is only the normal
reaction of children who did not
get the support they needed at an
earlier stage.

Although teenagers still need guidance in life, if they have not developed a sense of self they feel huge urges to do just the opposite of whatever is your will and wish.

# The Pressure of Parenting

To be secure children should feel heard, but always know that they are not the boss.

Parenting pushes you beyond the limits of how much you thought you could give.

Even with a greater understanding of the five messages of positive parenting, being a good parent is not easy. It is a learn-as-you-go process.

Parenting requires a tremendous commitment on our part but our children are certainly worth it.

Always remember that no one can do it better than you can. Although your children come from heaven they also come from you, and they need you.

Parenting is a difficult job, but it is also the most rewarding. To be a parent is an awesome responsibility and a great honour.

It doesn't work to treat children
as if they are good and innocent
and then spank them for being bad
a week later.

We can't always give our
children what they need or want
but we can help them respond to
their disappointments in healthy
ways that make them stronger and
more confident.

By fully committing yourself to the new principles of positive parenting you are a courageous pioneer exploring new territory, a brave hero creating a new world and, most important, you are giving your children the opportunities for greatness that you never had.

If we want our children to feel good about themselves we have to stop making them feel bad.

Using the five messages of positive parenting, and remembering that children are from heaven, will help you give your children the best preparation they could have to make all their dreams come true, which is what all parents want for their children.

If we want our children to respect others we must learn how to show them the respect they deserve.

Both our ability to create outer success and our ability to be happy and fulfilled are heavily influenced by early childhood circumstances and conditions.

Children learn by example. If you manage them with violence they will resort to violence, or at least sometimes cruel or insensitive behaviour when they don't know what else to do.

As parents we don't have to give more, instead we need an approach different from that of our parents.

With an increased knowledge of the importance of childhood, parents today feel much greater pressure and responsibility to find the best way to parent their children.

As in other areas of life, more is not always better.

Parents commonly make the mistake of focusing too much on providing more, but what they are providing more of is often counterproductive: more money, more toys, more entertainment, more education, more after-school activities, more praise, more time, more responsibility, more freedom, more discipline, more supervision, more punishment, more permission.

Today we are faced with the challenge of reinventing parenting.

Within every child are the seeds of greatness. Our role is to provide a safe and nurturing environment to give that child a chance to develop and express his or her potential.

Traditional parenting skills and approaches that were appropriate in the past will not work for children today.

Positive parenting is a shift from fear-based to love-based parenting.

Positive parenting focuses on new approaches and strategies to motivate children with love, not through the fear of punishment, humiliation or the loss of love.

Managing our children with fear, no matter how much we don't want to do it, is an automatic reaction.

# Love-based Parenting

Love-based parenting focuses on motivating children to co-operate without using the fear of punishment. When we feel out of control or are afraid of losing control this approach is in conflict with our deepest instinctive reactions.

Giving up spanking, threatening and punishing may sound like a loving thing to do, but when your child is throwing a tantrum in the check-out queue, and you just don't know what else to do, threatening or spanking seems to be the only solution.

When your child refuses to get dressed for school in the morning, or resists brushing his teeth at night, you automatically resort to threats and punishment.

Even if you don't want to use threats and punishment, when nothing else works it is all you have. And because you haven't yet learned the skills of positive parenting it is all you have.

If we are to give up spanking and punishing we must replace them with something that works effectively to manage children and create co-operation.

Children who are severely beaten or abused will bond with the abuser and defend the abusive behaviour.

There is no doubt that when children are managed by using the threat of violence, punishment or guilt, they will resort to violence, punishment or guilt when they feel out of control as a way to regain control.

Children exposed to violence either hate others or hate themselves.

When children are not over-stimulated by violence or meanness on TV they are clearly more secure, relaxed and peaceful.

Children learn primarily by imitation. What they see is what they do. Too much sensory input overwhelms their nervous system and they become irritable, demanding, moody, hyper, whiny, too sensitive and uncooperative. Too much stimulation is not a healthy influence.

When children are raised to believe they are bad and they deserve punishment, violence on TV and in films has a much greater negative impact.

In girls, aggressive tendencies are acted out against themselves with feelings of low self-esteem and eating disorders.

When children are over-stimulated by aggression or the threat of punishment at home, it creates hyperactivity in boys – or what is now diagnosed as Attention Deficit Disorder.

You can't give children more freedom unless you have the skills to restrain them so that they behave in an orderly manner.

Giving up past fear-based techniques only works when you replace them with something else that is more effective.

Positive parenting uses the practice of making the child take time out in a variety of ways which are age appropriate. This replaces the need to spank or punish.

No one ever deserves punishment. Everyone deserves to be loved and supported. Even in the past no one ever deserved punishment, but it was the only way to regain and maintain control.

In the past punishment maintained control, but today it has the opposite effect.

Just as society has changed, so have our children. Our children will not be broken but will continue to rebel in response to spanking and punishment.

The attributes of love, compassion, co-operation and forgiveness are no longer lofty concepts for philosophers and spiritual leaders, they are daily experiences.

All parents want their children to know what is right and then, on that basis, to act wisely.

If you are still against giving up spanking and punishing ask yourself this question: If there was another way to have the same or an even better effect that didn't involve fear, punishment or guilt, would I consider it?

Rather than focus on teaching children what is right and wrong, positive parenting is more focused on awakening and developing children's innate ability to know within themselves what is right and what is wrong.

Every child born today has the innate ability to know what is right and wrong. They have the potential to develop a conscience, but that ability must be nurtured if it is to come out.

Children respect others, not out of fear but because it feels good. They are willing to and capable of negotiating. They can think for themselves.

Positive-parenting practices
awaken that inner potential in our
children. The result of being
connected to an inner conscience is
that our children are well behaved
but not mindlessly obedient.

Connected children are willing
to challenge authority figures.
They are creative, co-operative,
competent, compassionate,
confident and loving.

There is no greater reward in life
than seeing your children succeed
in making their dreams come true
and feeling good about themselves.

# New Skills to Create Co-operation

Using "will" or "would" bypasses much of children's resistance and invites them to participate.

Although it sounds polite to use "could you" and "can you" to create co-operation, they are ineffective. To repeatedly use "could" and "can" sends confusing messages and gradually numbs children's natural willingness to co-operate.

Give up giving lectures.

Don't use feelings to manipulate.

Children need to experience that you are listening to them just as they are listening to you.

Repeated attempts to break a child's will undermines a child's natural willingness to co-operate.

By nurturing our children's need at times of resistance we can most effectively minimise resistance while keeping their will intact.

# FOUR SKILLS TO
# MINIMISE RESISTANCE

These are the four ways of nurturing:

1. Listening and understanding
2. Preparation and structure
3. Distraction and direction
4. Ritual and rhythm

To let go of their resistance and
feel their inner urge to co-operate,
children need understanding,
structure, direction and rhythm.

# The Four Temperaments

There are four different temperaments in children, which is why they sometimes respond better to one approach rather than another.

# SENSITIVE CHILDREN NEED LISTENING AND UNDERSTANDING

The first temperament is sensitive.
Sensitive children are more vulnerable,
dramatic and feeling. They respond
most to listening and understanding.

Sensitive children need empathy and validation of their pain and struggles.

The biggest mistake a parent can make is trying to cheer this child up.

# ACTIVE CHILDREN NEED PREPARATION AND STRUCTURE

The second temperament is active. Active children are concerned with doing, action and results. They are self-motivated and most co-operative when they know what to do or have a plan. They are always ready to move on, lead, or do things their way.

Active children always need
to know in advance what the
plan is, what the rules are and
who is the boss.

To minimise resistance make the
active child first, or put him or her
in charge of something.

Putting active children in a leadership role with clear guidelines brings out the best in them.

Active children need lots of acknowledgment for their successes and forgiveness for their mistakes.

Active children have a difficult time just sitting and listening. They need to move around and learn best by doing and participating with others.

Active children always want to be a part of the winning team.

# RESPONSIVE CHILDREN NEED DISTRACTION AND DIRECTION

The third temperament is responsive. Responsive children are social and outgoing. They are self-motivated to see, hear, taste and experience everything life has to offer. They have many interests because they have a greater need for stimulation.

Responsive children naturally move from one activity to another like a butterfly. They need time to explore, experience and discover life.

Responsive children know themselves by reacting to life's different experiences.

Without the right kind of support, responsive children, overwhelmed by life's responsibilities, tend to become easily irresponsible or overly scattered and they often reject the responsibilities of being an adult.

Responsive children tend to be more joyous, light and eager. They are literally fed by life's images and changes. For them life is an adventure. They tend to be more social and talk a lot. They make friends easily and tend to like everyone. They are often irresistible, charming and accommodating. They don't hold grudges.

# RECEPTIVE CHILDREN NEED RITUAL AND RHYTHM

The fourth temperament is receptive. Receptive children are the most good-natured and thoughtful children.

Receptive children participate
by observing.

Receptive children feel loved by
expecting it. Loving rituals need to
be created so that these children
have a way to experience their
worthiness and special connection
with each parent.

All repetitive behaviours, routines and rituals provide a sense of rhythm to life. We are comforted by knowing what is coming next. We are familiar with what is to be. All children need rhythm and ritual, but receptive children depend on it the most if they are to come out of their cocoon and express their inner gifts and talents.

As a rule, if there is a change they don't want it.

The activity of singing will distract many children of all ages from what is bothering them and redirect them to feeling loved and supported.

When children are distressed a simple song used over and over will distract them from their troubles and redirect them back to feeling loved and comforted.

When a child is restless and fussy before going to bed, besides singing little songs, reading stories is an excellent way to prepare the child to relax peacefully and sleep deeply.

By hearing stories children are easily distracted from life's burdens. Children use images created by hearing stories to develop their imagination, creativity and a stronger sense of self.

Let your child take time to develop and he or she will easily adapt to the real world when ready.

Children live in the eternal now. When a chore takes too long it feels like, "Work is all we ever do." By making chores easier and helping your children more they will learn first how to have fun, and then later in life, as teenagers, schoolwork will be more enjoyable.

It is the parents' job to give and the child's job to receive.

# New Skills to Minimise Resistance

The most important skills for minimising resistance and creating co-operation are listening and understanding. When children resist co-operating some part of them is wanting or needing something else.

Understanding your child's
resistance is enough to make
it go away.

When children resist a parent
it is often because they are
wanting something else. They
assume that if you just understood,
you would want to support their
want, wish or need.

The power of understanding your children's resistance is that it immediately minimises resistance. When children get the message that you understand what they want and how important it is to them, then their resistance level changes.

Children resist their parents simply because they don't feel heard or seen.

Taking a few extra minutes to listen and identify children's feelings, wants, wishes and needs will not only give them what they really need but also give parents more time for their own needs.

Taking the time to listen is much more important than getting to soccer practice on time.

When children are not given permission to resist, frustration builds up inside and comes out when the parent is most distressed. This problem can be averted by taking time, when you do have the time, to listen to your children's resistance. Give them the message again and again that they are seen and heard.

All children can benefit from distraction. Up to about eight years old children are easily distracted from their resistance by being told a little story with lots of imagery, colour and shapes.

To minimise resistance, establish rapport and then invite participation.

At any age, when children are upset
and resistant they respond well to
redirection like, "Now let's do this ..."
or "And now we will ..." Rather than
ask the child what she wants to do,
or even what she would like to do,
the parent needs to lead the child.

To communicate that you hear
or understand a child's pressing
needs, wishes and wants, two
conditions must be met.

If you never have time to listen
you are not giving your children
what they require. An ounce
of prevention is worth a pound of
cure. Don't wait until children's
resistance builds up and
then explodes.

Under children's resistance are first
anger, then sadness and then fear.

When it comes to dealing with
our children's resistance there are
generally two different approaches:
soft love and hard love.

Hard-love parents mistakenly
believe, "If I tolerate my children's
resistance I will spoil them. They
must always remember
who is boss."

It's time to update and adjust the old adage, "Spare the rod and spoil the child."

The hard-love approach teaches children who is boss, but does not tolerate children's natural resistance.

Punishment may make them obedient in the short term, but later on they will rebel.

This rebellion not only makes parenting more time-consuming, difficult and painful, it obstructs a child's natural development.

The huge disconnection that is occurring today between parents and teenagers is not healthy – it is just common.

In raising merely obedient
children we fail to give them
the winning edge.

Success in life doesn't come from
following rules it comes from
thinking for oneself and following
one's heart and inner will.
This natural ability is first nurtured
by strengthening a child's
willingness to co-operate.

When parents are able to respond to a child's resistance calmly, without threats of punishment or disapproval, then the child gradually learns how to deal with the resistance she experiences in the world.

Positive parenting teaches children to navigate through life's obstacles with understanding and great negotiation skills.

Many parents have given up hard parenting. They recognise the importance of listening but don't understand the importance of being the boss.

This brand of soft-love parenting does not work and has made many parents suspicious of new nurturing skills of positive parenting.

The failure of soft-love parenting makes many parents suspicious of positive-parenting techniques.

Soft-love parents sometimes give in to their child's wants and wishes, because they just don't know what else to do to stop the tantrum.

Soft-love parenting tries to please and placate the child. Soft-love parents will do whatever they can to avoid a confrontation with their child.

Giving choices will lessen resistance but it will not create co-operation.

Directly asking a young child what she wants puts too much pressure on the child. Always asking children what they want or how they feel weakens a parent's ability to maintain control.

Children younger than nine need strong parents who know what is best for them, but who are also open to hearing their resistance and discovering their wants and wishes.

99

Children need strong parents who know what is best; they don't need more choices.

Permissive soft parenting minimises resistance in the short term, but weakens children's willingness to co-operate.

Using positive-parenting skills means hearing your child's resistance and then deciding what is best.

As a result of hard parenting girls tend to lack confidence while boys lack compassion. As a result of soft parenting girls tend to have low self-esteem and, later in life, give too much, while boys become hyperactive and lack confidence and discipline.

There is a world of difference between giving in to your child's feelings or wishes and changing what you think should be done. Parents are the boss, but they must not always rigidly hold on to their request or point of view. To listen to a child's resistance means to consider what he or she is feeling and wanting, and to decide what is best and then to persist.

Learning to accept the boundaries and limits of time and space is a big lesson in life. Pushing up against life's limits can teach children to embrace those limits without having to deny themselves.

Many studies have shown that children who are able to postpone gratification are more successful in life.

Look around you and you will see that people who succeed are people who patiently persist in achieving their goals.

The ability to delay gratification is also the ability to be happy and at peace even though you don't have everything you want.

When children resist not getting what they want, and parents can identify and understand the feelings underlying the resistance and can communicate that understanding to them, then the children discover their natural ability to be happy and accepting even though they are not getting what they want.

Children need boundaries to push up against. When they don't get them they are restless and insecure. When they get their way too often, what they get is never enough. It is only when we are feeling our needs that we can appreciate what we get.

You can't always give your children what they want but you can give them what they really need. If you don't focus on providing what they need, you and your children suffer increasing resistance.

By expressing and then letting
go of resistance children learn to
accept what has to be.

When children don't know what
to do they often forget how you
want them to behave.

# New Skills for Increasing Motivation

Most parents don't want to punish their children, they just don't know another way that works.

By feeling pain we are automatically induced to correct our thoughts and actions.

The ability to know right from wrong comes from our feelings. Feelings, whether negative (pain) or positive (pleasure), help us to make necessary adjustments.

Our children today have a greater potential and require a new and different kind of support.

When parents raise children with open hearts, minds, and strong free wills this quiet voice is not some exalted experience that only saints can hear but a common experience motivating children's daily behaviour.

The more children feel nurtured and loved the more confusing punishment is. We cannot nurture our children and open their minds and hearts to be strong, creative and capable, only to turn around and threaten them like animals.

Instead of motivating children with punishment, children today need to be motivated with rewards.

It is more damaging to open up children and then punish them than to ignore their feelings and wants, occasionally punishing them to maintain control.

If we are to give our children the opportunity to open up their minds and hearts and develop a strong will we must learn another way to motivate other than punishment.

Children who are not punished
are often unruly, undisciplined
and disrespectful to each other
and to adults and teachers. Yet
every parent, at some time, has felt
in their quiet moments that there
must be a different way.

The promise of more
inspires everyone, old or young,
to co-operate.

For some, motivating their children with a reward somehow implies that they as parents are weak and that their children are running the show.

The first and most important reason children today misbehave is that they are not getting what they need to stay in touch with their inner feelings.

Children today just need understanding, structure, direction and rhythm. Then they will automatically be more in touch with their feelings.

Children go out of control when they are not getting what they need.

The second reason a child misbehaves is determined by how the parent deals with the child's unruly behaviour.

When you punish a child a lot of attention gets put on a child's negative behaviour.

If you reward a child's positive behaviour, that is what will increase.

Rather than look for and focus on children's mistakes, try to "catch" them doing things right.

Have a neutral to bored attitude regarding mistakes and focus on enthusiasm and positive feelings when regarding their successes.

By pointing out and acknowledging positive things about your children and their behaviour they will see themselves as successful and good.

Resistance is inevitable because parents are not perfect and cannot always give children what they need.

Rather than mistakenly assuming that our children don't want to co-operate we need to realise that they don't have what they need to co-operate.

The purpose of rewarding children is to awaken the part of them that wants to co-operate.

Instead of trying to get control with threats of punishment or spanking, at those times when our children resist co-operating we can regain co-operation by means of rewards.

In many cases a child's resistance just melts away with a reward. With occasional rewards a child is reconnected with her natural desire to please the parent, and she automatically co-operates more of the time.

Giving small rewards makes parenting so much easier.

Ideally a reward is the natural
consequence of co-operation.
If the child brushes her teeth right
away there is more time to read
stories before bedtime.

To motivate co-operation the
easiest reward to give is more
time with you.

Whenever your child co-operates
the real consequence is more time
later to do something they would
really like to do with you.

To make your reward even
more effective try to communicate
it in ways that appeal more to
your child.

# Rewards According to Temperaments

With a more sensitive child, when describing the reward focus on how it will feel. For example, "If you co-operate with me now I will have more time to do something special later. We could have fun picking flowers for Mummy in the garden."

With an active child, when describing a reward focus more on the details of action. "If you co-operate with me now I will have more time to do something special later."

With a responsive child, when describing the reward focus more on the sensory details and tell a story. For example, "If you co-operate with me now I will have more time to do something special later. We could go out in the garden and pick the beautiful flowers for Mummy."

With a receptive child, when describing the reward focus more on the timing. For example, say, "If you co-operate with me now, I will have more time to do something special later. After school, when we come home we can pick flowers in the garden for Mummy."

While framing the reward in different ways for your particular child will increase your child's motivation, just communicating the reward will still work.

What makes giving rewards work is finding things that really motivate your children.

The secret of giving rewards is to pay attention to the things your children want most and use these to reward them.

The very things you would take away to punish can instead be given as rewards.

Prepared parents always have a few rewards up their sleeve to pull out when their child is resisting.

A wise parent attempts to think ahead and prepare children for changes.

The real magic of rewards is that, at times when nothing seems to work, promising a reward will work. Without this clear insight and skill positive parenting cannot succeed. Without the alternative of making a deal with your children through promising a reward, the only recourse is to threaten them with a punishment.

Children are more co-operative if
we recognise what is difficult for
them and give a little more because
they co-operated.

If your child throws a tantrum
in a public place, recognise that
you don't have the time to give
the child what he or she needs
to be more co-operative.

You can remedy the situation by
quickly offering your child a reward
for co-operating.

Even though this is placating the child, if only done occasionally it is fine.

When children are uncooperative in public it is a warning sign to be tougher at home and not placate so much.

Next time prepare your child by letting him know that you realise it is more difficult to be co-operative the check-out queue. Let him know that you don't like waiting in long queues either. Then make a deal. Say something like this, "If you co-operate with Mummy we will have time to come home and have a bowl of your favourite cereal."

When you offer children a reward you are helping them once again connect to the part of themselves that wants to help. A reward doesn't make them co-operate. Instead it is another way to nurture a child's natural motivation.

Appropriately rewarding our children prepares them to think of both themselves and others.

It is important for our children to learn that life is a process of give and take. If you give then you get. To get more you give more.

For many parents there is an implied assumption that children who don't co-operate are bad. They mistakenly believe that good children automatically co-operate.

Positive parenting recognises
that when children don't co-operate
they are not bad, they are just not
getting what they need. At times
of resistance, a parent is required
either to give them what they
need or to use rewards to motivate
them in that moment.

Positive parenting doesn't require fear to motivate children to remember.

Leave natural consequences up to nature; don't play God.

# New Skills for Asserting Leadership

Parents need to command their children. In a firm but calm voice tell them what you want them to do.

Once you use your command voice you must remain strong. Using emotions, reasons, explanations and arguments, blame or threats weakens your natural authority.

The most powerful assertiveness technique is to repeat your command with the confidence that the child will soon yield.

A clear and firm command repeated over and over without the tone of emotional distress is most effective.

Children don't need perfect parents but they do need parents who do their best and take responsibility for their mistakes.

When you don't hold it against them they won't hold it against you.

Command but don't explain.
Giving reasons is a way of giving
up your command.

Children learn right from wrong
by co-operating with your requests,
not by listening to your lectures.

"Because I am the parent, that's
why" is the best response to
children's challenge to commands.

# New Skills for Maintaining Control

Under stress children go out of control, like a speeding car without a driver.

Time outs are needed to regain
control when emotions become
too strong.

A wise adult knows when to take
time out and a child doesn't.

A frustrated, demanding
parent can easily spin a child
out of control.

When a child is not willing to co-operate, a time out is an opportunity for the child to blow off steam and throw a tantrum.

Within a few short minutes of time out all the emotional drama suddenly lifts away.

As children co-operate they
automatically learn what is right
or wrong, good or bad.

Giving time outs replaces the
outdated need to punish or
spank children.

The ideal time out is when a parent puts a child in another room and holds the door shut.

The time needed is one minute for each year. A four-year-old stays in the room for four minutes. It works for all children and all ages from two years old.

Reassure your child that you are just on the other side of the door and that they will soon be able to come out.

Time outs are to be used as a last resort.

If a child just laughs and ignores you, then clearly this child is out of control.

If your child needs more time outs it doesn't mean something is wrong with your child or your parenting approach.

With regular time outs children learn to manage their inner feelings.

It is not giving children more that spoils them, it is giving them more to avoid confrontation.

Sometimes a child just needs
a good cry to feel better.

The absence of acceptance
manifests itself in the statement:
"Something is wrong with
my child."

Being different doesn't mean one style is better than another.

Caring motivates parents to be involved, interested and affected by children's experiences of life.

Trust motivates a parent to give freedom and space for children to do things for themselves.

Regardless of age, boys tend
to need trust more while girls
need caring.

The challenge for parents is to
give a girl extra doses of caring,
understanding and respect so that
she can continue trusting.

When a girl is neglected it is often too painful to continue needing and in reaction she becomes more masculine.

The challenge for parents regarding a boy is to give extra doses of trust, acceptance and appreciation to keep him motivated.

Offering help to a girl may make her feel cared for, but a boy may take it as an insult.

When a boy is smothered with caring he may react by becoming more needy.

The most common mistake
mothers make is to offer
unsolicited advice when children
misbehave, make mistakes or
appear to need help.

Women realise that no matter
how good it gets it can always
get better.

When a mother worries too much, or offers too much advice, it smothers children with caring and deprives them of the trust they need.

For every correction, catch your child doing something right three times.

It is not that advice is wrong. When children are clearly asking for advice it is very helpful. The big problem is that mothers give too much advice and, as a result, their children stop listening.

Understanding differences helps us to understand and support our children better.

Under stress, boys become more focused while girls need to talk more. Women often misunderstand this difference and misinterpret a man's forgetfulness as not caring.

Taking away freedom is not the solution, but strengthening the bond of communication is.

Today, more than ever, teenagers need clear and open lines of communication with their parents. The challenges that our teenagers face are enormous. Without parental support it is extremely difficult not to be swayed by negative influences.

When teenagers do not feel accepted at home they seek acceptance from their peers.

Be open-minded and your children
will be free to make their choices
instead of just rebelling.

To support our children we must
hold back advice, rigid judgments
and solutions in order to keep the
lines of communication open.

## DIFFERENT TEMPERAMENTS

As we have explored, there are basically four temperaments: sensitive, active, responsive and receptive.

1. Sensitive children have stronger feelings, go deeper and are more serious.

2. Active children have strong wills, take risks and want to be the centre of attention.

3. Responsive children are bright, light and need more stimulation;

they move from one thing to
another.

4. Receptive children are well
   mannered and co-operative; they
   follow instructions well but
   resist change.

Unless parents are aware of all
four temperaments it is very
difficult to nurture a child whose
temperament differs from theirs.

The risk of failure may hold children back from learning new skills.

Children younger than nine are not capable of dealing with shaming messages without assuming too much blame.

It does no good at all to focus
on a child's mistake.

Those who succeed in life are those
who can self-correct and change
their thinking, attitude or behaviour.

If children feel afraid of making mistakes, they lose the natural ability to self-correct.

When children take longer to learn it is neither their fault nor the parents', it is just what is required.

By being guided again and again
to do the right thing children
eventually learn what is right.

Focusing on mistakes does not
serve children in any way.

Many parents mistakenly
expect the sense of responsibility
of a nineteen-year-old from a
young child.

There is always the chance in
life to re-balance the scales when
a mistake or wrongdoing
has occurred.

Instead of explaining why they were late, parents should listen, apologise and make amends.

Parents can teach their children to be responsible by demonstrating responsibility.

Positive-parenting skills do not use any punishments to motivate co-operation, but sometimes a parent may have to make adjustments regarding certain freedoms given to a child or teenager.

When a teenager is consistently late adjust the curfew to an earlier time.

When your child breaks a vase, regardless of the circumstances, she deserves a forgiving response.

When children make a mistake it is the worst time to remind them of other mistakes they have made.

Don't put much attention on children's mistakes.

Punishment or getting upset with your child are out-dated ways to communicate. The best kind of reaction to your child's mistakes is a kind of neutral or bored look.

When children fail or make mistakes, parents incorrectly assume that they are not doing their best.

Positive parenting recognises that children are always doing their best.

When making mistakes is not acceptable children react in a variety or unhealthy ways. The following list contains four common ways our children react when their mistakes are not accepted:

1. Hiding mistakes and not telling the truth.

2. Not setting high standards or taking risks.

3. Defending themselves by justifying mistakes or blaming others.

4. Low self-esteem and self-punishment.

Children learn to love themselves
by the way they are treated and
by the way parents react to
their mistakes.

When children hide a mistake
a part of themselves is unable
to let love in.

Living in a comfort zone, children not only sell themselves short but also become bored.

Parents mistakenly think they are helping when they give shaming messages.

Natural tendencies to hold back
are magnified when children get
unforgiving messages.

As long as we justify our mistakes
by blaming someone else we
cannot self-correct.

When it is okay to make mistakes, instead of defending, children are open to listening.

Children may be very good in their behaviour, but at the cost of their self-esteem.

Children feel okay when parents feel everything is okay.

When children are punished for
mistakes they continue to feel the
fear throughout their lives.

Shaming or punishing children for
being upset subdues their passions
and breaks their will.

Parents must be careful not to placate a child to avoid having to deal with a tantrum.

The most important element of learning to manage negative emotions is first to make them acceptable.

Unsuccessful people are either numb to their inner feelings or remain struck in negative feelings and attitudes.

Negative emotions are always okay, but they must be expressed at the appropriate time and place.

It is not acceptable for a child to dominate the family with demanding emotional tantrums. Parents must be strong, but at the same time create opportunities for children to have the tantrums they need to have.

When children are upset, from their perspective there are always valid reasons.

Getting in touch with feelings makes us more aware of who we are, what we need, wish and want.

Empathy is that magic switch that opens children up to receiving reassurance and guidance.

When children throw tantrums
they have temporarily forgotten
who is the boss and the importance
of being loved.

What our children need most is
silent understanding, caring and a
little expressed validation.

Giving empathy sometimes only requires a few extra seconds of silent caring and understanding.

When your children stop listening to you, it is clearly because you have been giving too much advice.

When children resist try to remember that this is the time when they need you to listen to them.

Negative emotions tend to stimulate emotional reactions in others. When someone is sad we feel sad. When someone is angry with us we often feel anger in return.

When they express negative emotions, parents are bigger, louder and more powerful and intimidate children.

Strong adult emotions make it unsafe for children to feel.

To help our children manage their feelings we must also manage our own feelings.

It is very unhealthy for children to feel responsible for their parents' feelings.

Children should never get the
message that they are responsible
for how a parent feels.

Parents can successfully
communicate that they have
feelings by telling stories
from their past.

Let this guide help you on your journey. May your children grow up confident, co-operative and compassionate. May they always experience lasting love in their family and friends.